WRIGHT

T0018613

WRIGHT

NAOMI STUNGO

Frank Lloyd Wright | Never has an architect combined genius and infamy with such staggering aplomb as the American Frank Lloyd Wright. The model for numerous books, plays and films, including Ayn Rand's study of megalomania *The Fountainhead* (1943), Wright designed more than 1,000 buildings during his prolific ninety-two-year lifetime, scandalized polite society continually with his outrageous private life and declared himself not only the single-handed founder of modern architecture but also the greatest architect – ever.

How you decide who is the world's greatest architect is far from clear. How can you compare Michelangelo against the very different talent of Gaudí? What is to be gained by comparing Brunelleschi with Alvar Aalto? Certainly, a number of Wright's buildings rank among the world's most famous; the Guggenheim Museum in New York and the waterside summer house in Pennsylvania known as Fallingwater are internationally acclaimed. And yet, much of his architecture has huge technical faults. Many of his buildings have leaked since the day they were completed and Fallingwater had to be shored up or it would have, literally, fallen into the water. So was Wright the inventor of modern architecture? Well, maybe. In his pioneering use of open-plan living areas, his "honest" expression of materials, his interest in technology and respect for nature, Wright anticipated almost all of the key themes that dominated architecture in the twentieth century.

Born in Wisconsin in 1867, Frank Lincoln Wright – as he was christened – was the eldest child and only son of William Wright, a local minister and music teacher, and his wife Anna Lloyd Jones Wright. His strong-willed mother was a passionate and ambitious woman who channelled the frustrations of her unhappy marriage into pushing her young son. She had a formative influence over Wright: not only did he take her name as a teenager when his parents divorced, but Wright credited her with determining the very direction of his life, claiming that his mother had told him of a premonition she had while pregnant with him – her son was to become a great architect.

Previous page. Taliesin East, the Wisconsin estate of Frank Lloyd Wright. **Above.** The architect with a model of his St Mark's Tower – an eighteen-storey apartment building made entirely of glass, steel and concrete. Based on a tetradic plan, the project was abandoned in 1929 but resurfaced as the Price Tower in Bartlesville, Oklahoma, in 1956.

Above. The Taliesin 3 table lamp, here shown in the Bethesda home of the architect's grandson, Tom Wright, shows the influence of the Froebel system.

Whether or not this is true, and it smacks rather of the myth that Wright later built up around his life, Anna Wright certainly encouraged her son's early interest in architecture, decorating his nursery with prints of English cathedrals and teaching him to play with Froebel blocks. A teacher herself, she was fascinated by these new toys – coloured strips of paper, two-dimensional geometric grids, wood spheres, blocks and pyramids – which were designed by the German educational philosopher Friedrich Froebel, the inventor of the kindergarten. The toys, used in conjunction with a series of elaborate exercises, were intended to develop children's sensory experience of the world and seemed to have a profound effect on Wright. "I give you my word," Wright used to say, describing their effect on his thinking, "all those things are in my hands today – the feeling of those maple forms." Looking at Wright's architecture you see the Froebel shapes – the cube, the sphere, the pyramid and myriad combinations of all of them – recurring time and again. "There," he explained, "is the modular system that has been back [sic] of every design I ever made."

The Froebel system was more, however, than a mere set of spatial and analytical exercises; Froebel intended the toys to have symbolic and spiritual meaning. As environmental historian William Cronon has explained, Froebel believed that certain key geometric forms symbolized human ideas, moods and sentiments: the circle, infinity; the triangle, structural unity; the spire, aspiration; the spiral, organic progress; the square, integrity. It sounds strange today but the idea that a set of toys could teach children about the underlying principles of the cosmos was far from outlandish in the mid-nineteenth century. For Anna Wright, and later her son, the idea had huge appeal, tying in as it did with their Unitarian beliefs.

To understand Frank Lloyd Wright, you have to understand something of Unitarianism, the religion in which his family was steeped through and through. Wright's father was a Unitarian preacher, his mother descended from a long line of Welsh Unitarians who had settled in Wisconsin in the 1840s. Extreme liberal Protestants, they rejected almost every convention of the established church, stressing instead reason and conscience as the foundations of religion. Individuals, they believed, should seek out God for themselves in the world around them. The function of science and art was to help in this quest

I think Nature should be spelled with a capital "N", not because Nature is God but because all that we can learn of God we will learn from the body of God which we call Nature. Frank Lloyd Wright, lecture at Sarah Lawrence College, New York, 1958

– hence children's toys should be vehicles for understanding the underlying principles of the universe and the nature of God.

Another important vehicle for Wright was the natural world itself. Nature is a key theme in Wright's thinking, and we see it recalled again and again in his designs – in decorative motifs such as stained glass, furnishings and fittings, as well as in his more general concern to site his buildings in harmony with their natural surroundings, as if they had grown naturally from them. From nature, he learned to simplify his designs. And like a living thing, even small individual parts in a Wright building typically relate to the whole.

He was further inspired by that most American of philosophies: transcendentalism. Ralph Waldo Emerson, who was once an ordained Unitarian minister, espoused the values of individualism and the creation of a unique American culture that eschewed European heritage. For Wright, true democracy was a community of individuals who had the freedom to think and act creatively, the reverse of the "mobocracy" that he associated with the metropolis. ("Cities force growth and make men talkative and entertaining," wrote Emerson, "but they make them artificial" – or, one might say, *un*natural.) Henry David Thoreau's emphasis on simplicity and self-sufficiency would be echoed in Wright's insistence on "the elimination of the nonessential", while Thoreauvian non-conformism became Wright's stock-in-trade. The poet Walt Whitman was another spiritual kinsman, and his concept of an Absolute Self – that each individual is but a small component of the great mass of souls – chimed with Emerson's idea of the Over-Soul and Wright's use of architectural details to serve as a microcosm of a whole building. "I celebrate myself, and sing myself," begins Whitman's famous declaration "Song of Myself" (1855), "And what I assume you shall assume / For every atom belonging to me as good belongs to you." And Whitman's identification of spaciousness as integral to Americanness became one of Wright's core beliefs.

Wright's formal architectural training began at the age of eighteen when he enrolled in the engineering school at the University of Wisconsin in Madison. Ambitious and impatient in equal measure, he soon tired of small-town life. For a young man passionate about architecture, Chicago was clearly the only place to be, the melting pot of technology and design. When Wright arrived in 1887, the city was in the throes of a building bonanza: the great fire of 1871 had destroyed huge swathes of the city, which were now being rebuilt on a heroic scale thanks to the invention of the elevator a few years earlier by Elisha Graves Otis.

Wright quickly sought out the most innovative architectural practice, Adler and Sullivan, where despite his lack of experience he was taken on as an assistant to Louis Sullivan. Here began one of the most formative experiences of Wright's long life. For, although they were later to fall out, Wright always recognized Sullivan as an exemplary teacher, referring to him as his *Lieber Meister* or "Dear Master". Certainly it was an exciting office to work in: when Wright joined the practice, Adler and Sullivan were engaged on the Auditorium Building, one of the most famous tall buildings of its time. Wright progressed quickly and was soon put in charge of the practice's residential work, so beginning his lifelong passion for house design.

Wright honed his early style in a succession of remarkable houses built in the smart Chicago suburb of Oak Park. Like his *Lieber Meister*, Wright sought to create a new and authentic American architecture. Rejecting the then fashionable Classical Beaux-Arts style, he set about developing an architecture in keeping with the vast expanses of the Midwest.

Above. Walter Gale House, Oak Park, Illinois, 1893.
Opposite. Frank Lloyd Wright Home and Studio, Oak Park, Illinois, 1889.

The first hints of this Prairie style, as it became known, appear in the Oak Park house that Wright designed for himself and his first wife, Catherine Lee Tobin. The couple married in 1889 and, borrowing money from Sullivan, Wright began the house that was to be home to himself, Catherine and their six children for the next ten years.

With its low, ground-hugging proportions, horizontal emphasis and free-flowing interior spaces, the house was a radical departure from the mock Tudor and steep roofs of most American suburbs. What were effectively free-standing partitions served to divide up the more or less unbroken spaces on the main floor. And the core, the kitchen and fireplace, set back to back, from which the rest of the house symbolically expands, was something that foreshadowed the architect's interest in radial plans. His astonishing ability to synthesize detail and theme across an entire scheme is already evident. Take the dining room, where he designed the

Above. Winslow House, Illinois, 1894.

furniture, ceiling light (filtered via a wooden grillwork dense with circular forms) and cabinets enclosing the radiators.

Wright's solo career was abruptly launched in 1893, when Sullivan fired him for moonlighting. Hurriedly adding a drafting studio to the house, Wright quickly picked up commissions from wealthy Chicagoans fleeing the Windy City for the tranquil greenery of Oak Park. He was still only twenty-six when he designed the Winslow House (1894), his first solo commission and the first true Prairie house.

When Daniel Burnham, the patriarch of Chicago architecture at the time, saw the Winslow House, he offered to send Wright on a study trip to the École des Beaux-Arts in Paris and on a grand tour of Italy. Burnham felt the house, while skilful, made no sense. Others agreed, even those with confidence in Wright. Indeed, his next client, Nathan G. Moore, came to him demanding a house as different from the Winslow House as possible, because he "[didn't] want to go down the backstreets to [his] morning train to avoid being laughed at".

Starkly unadorned, the Winslow House was revolutionary. Its low, hovering form rises directly from a raised plinth, so that the building seems to grow out of the ground. Instead of being covered in plaster, the cast concrete and brick are left bare, capped by a terracotta frieze, a gently oversailing roof and massive central chimney. The frontage is strongly horizontal, with an expanse of golden Roman brick distinguishing the lower part of the wall, contrasting strongly with the darker band of ornate tiling at the second storey. The emphatic symmetry and the ornamented masonry that surrounds the front door and bears an intricate oak-leaf motif are reminiscent of Sullivan's style, but the overall pointedly lateral feel is clearly Wright's. The house is further distinguished by its emphasis on the hearth as the centrepiece of the home. Step inside and you're faced with an inglenook, fronted with a row of slim arched columns, and – emphasizing its importance – slightly elevated from the foyer's floor.

And yet the impetus for this new aesthetic was surely not all American. In 1893, Wright had visited the Ho-o-den (Phoenix Hall) exhibit at the World's Columbian Exposition, a reconstructed Japanese temple. His reaction is not known, but the parallels between the flowing interior spaces, screen-like walls, overhanging eaves and long, low roofs of Japanese architecture and Wright's emerging Prairie style are too striking to ignore. In later life, he was certainly an avid Japanophile, living and working in the country and amassing a valuable collection of Japanese art, so it seems legitimate to speculate that an interest in things Japanese was partly responsible for the increasingly unorthodox style of his work.

In the Unity Temple (1908), the Unitarian chapel he designed for Oak Park, Wright experimented still further. The building comprises the temple itself and a second space, Unity House, for socializing, joined together by a narrow "neck" that also incorporates the entrance. It is shockingly blank-looking from the outside – and, eschewing European traditions (Emerson would have been delighted), had no steeple – although highly innovative in construction. Wright used reinforced concrete, poured on site, a technique commonly used to build warehouse and factories, but not places of worship. This had the added benefit of allowing decorative features to be cast in, rather than added later at additional expense – which would have further squeezed the modest $45,000 budget. "Unity Temple makes an entirely new architecture – and is the first expression of it," he later claimed. "That is my contribution to modern architecture."

In contrast to its plain shell, the temple's perfectly square interior is alive with light and movement, in keeping with Wright's belief that "The essence of organic building is space, space flowing outward, space flowing inward." Pushing what he called the "destruction of the box" – the replacement of the boxy layout of most nineteenth-century buildings with a more free-flowing arrangement – Wright supported the weight of the building's immense glazed roof on four huge columns. Balconies housing pews extend into the main volume of the space at different heights. As the high walls were non-load-

Above. Unity Temple, Illinois, 1908.

bearing, they could be used as screens, pierced with high-level stained-glass windows that – in tandem with the amber-tinted, coffered skylights – allow washes of light to play over the room.

The decoration is emphatically geometric – recurring squares and rectangles arranged as long strips of flat trim. (The shapes are deployed, at various scales, and both ornamentally and structurally, throughout the building.) They're strongly evocative of later designs by architects and architects associated with the Dutch De Stijl movement, such as Gerrit Rietveld, Robert van 't Hoff and J. J. P. Oud, who found inspiration in Wright's resolve to pare away established European architectural traditions – which chimed with their own aims – in his quest for a distinctively American vernacular. Van 't Hoff visited Wright in the USA in 1914, and his Villa Henny (1916) at Huis ter Heide directly references the master in its flat roof, dominant rectangular form, overhanging eaves and radial interior plan.

> We of the Middle West are living on the prairie. The prairie has a beauty of its own and we should recognize and accentuate this natural beauty, its quiet level. Hence, gently sloping roofs, low proportions, quiet sky lines, suppressed heavy-set chimneys and sheltering overhangs, low terraces ...
> Frank Lloyd Wright, *Architectural Record*, 1908

The "plasticity" of the Wrightian space, its disavowal of boxy forms, use of modern materials such as reinforced concrete and the architect's enthusiasm for the possibilities offered by the machine age, set him on a course parallel to that followed by De Stijl and other contemporary modernist movements. As early as 1901, in his lecture "The Art and Craft of the Machine", Wright praised

Above. Robie House, Illinois, 1910.

mechanization as a means of bringing about a new architecture of precision-tooled "clean, strong forms" with less waste and at lower cost.

The Robie House (1910) is the apotheosis of Wright's new, radical style. Hailed as the "house of the century" by *House and Home* magazine when threatened with demolition in 1958, it dissolves all interior space so that rooms become a string of pavilions linked by promenades and galleries. Massive and low, it became known, not surprisingly, as the "battleship". Piers at the eastern and western end of the house support most of the weight, via steel beams in the floors and ceilings, doing away with the need for internal columns. This frees up the outside walls for windows and doors, creating spacious rooms throughout and underlining Wright's preference for open-plan layouts.

To the south-west of the property, the deck-like lower floors house the playroom, billiard room and utility areas (at ground level), which flow seamlessly from one to the other. Above that lies the integrated dining and living rooms, which open to an outside balcony via French doors. In keeping with the nautical image, the living room represents a "prow" that opens to the west porch. The bedrooms are above on the smaller third floor – the "poop deck", as it were – on the north-east of the building; together with the heavy-set chimney, incorporating four fireplaces, it visually anchors the whole strange assembly. Art-glass panels decorate the windows on this floor; there are 174 of them in the house altogether, in twenty-nine different patterns. He'd used tinted glazing as early as his Oak Park home, whose studio features a densely patterned art-glass skylight, serving both as a decorative feature and as a means of diffusing light.

The main entrance is secluded to the north-west of the property, leaving the frontage free for those unbroken horizontal strata. It opens onto a hall with a low ceiling and limited lighting. The relative darkness makes what comes next all the more dramatic: at the top of the stairs, the second floor opens up into a space flooded with light.

Wright also designed the furniture, in keeping with his view of the house as one complete concept, effectively a *gesamtkunstwerk*. Extending the theme of openness to the dining-room table, for example, he added posts at the corners housing recessed vases and topped by lights so that guests and family would be able to see, uninterrupted, across its expanse. Elsewhere, a sofa incorporates extended armrests that serve as side tables. Stylistically, these mirror the house's cantilevered roof, which extends the building's horizontal sweep. Geometric and organic patterns on the windows pick up on others in the lights and carpets. That Wright not only designed the architecture of a house, but also aspects such as furnishings and window ornamentation, was unusual for the time and necessitated his working closely with glass and furniture producers to ensure the accurate translation of his unorthodox designs.

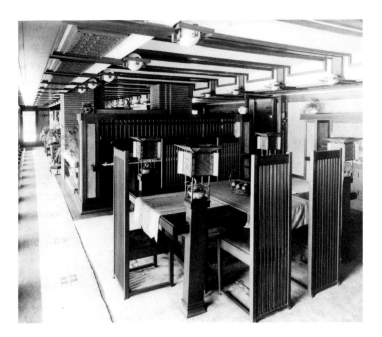

Above. Robie House, Illinois, 1910.

Only thirty-three years old when he commissioned Wright to design him a house, Frederick C. Robie was a talented young engineer and head of a company making bicycles. His house, he demanded, should run as smoothly as a machine. Looking at Wright's buildings today, it is difficult to imagine them as the pinnacle of technological achievement but, in their day, that is exactly what they were. For all his interest in nature, Wright was also a technocrat. The Robie House was the latest in fireproof houses, the Unity Temple used unpainted concrete as a cladding material for the first time, while the Larkin building pushed developments even further.

The Larkin Company Administration Building (1905) in Buffalo, New York, was demolished in 1950. If it were still standing today, it would be an astonishing sight. And what must have been thought of it at the time one can

Above. Larkin Company Administration Building, New York, 1905.

only wonder. The Larkin Building was a revolutionary machine for working in. Wright's client, a soap-making and mail-order tycoon, wanted a clean, delightful working environment that would foster good working relations between employer and employees. Wright rose to the task with a vengeance. Inside its cliff-like blank walls, the whole layout of the building was unique.

The dominant feature of the cream-brick interior was a central atrium that, lit from above, was wrapped around by four floors of open galleries so that everyone could see everyone – employer and employee alike. Wright had already employed ceiling skylights to similar effect for the Unity Temple, and here created a kind of secular cathedral to commerce, something that carried over into the inspirational inscriptions that lined the walls – "Co-operation,

Economy, Industry", "Intelligence, Enthusiasm, Control". It even accommodated a huge Möller pipe organ.

Sited at its corners, leaving cross-views unimpaired, were four shafts that brought in high-level fresh air, heated it and pumped it around the building. The building marked a series of "firsts": the steel desk furniture – with chairs suspended from tables, to make cleaning easier – the wall-hung toilets and the air-conditioning were all bespoke and utterly innovative. Magnesite cast concrete was used for features such as windowsills, partitions, floors, stairs and doors, helping to dampen sounds.

Wright was now famous: he was immensely prolific, his buildings were attracting widespread interest, he had clients aplenty, he was earning well. But he was bored and, in 1909, he threw it all in, abandoning his wife and six children for Mamah Cheney, the free-thinking feminist wife of a client and neighbour. Chicago society was scandalized and the pair fled to Europe. There began Wright's long wilderness years.

Not that the trip to Europe was unproductive. The couple travelled widely, visiting Vienna where Wright saw the work of the Secessionists; Berlin, where he published two editions of his work with the publisher Ernst Wasmuth; Italy and France. Returning to the USA in 1911, Wright had neither clients nor money and so set about building himself and Mrs Cheney a home in southern Wisconsin on land owned by his mother's family. He called the house Taliesin. Meaning "shining brow" in Welsh, a reference to the house's location on the crest of a hill, Taliesin was a retreat from the condemnatory world, a place of introspection and reflection, out of which the second great phase of Wright's career emerged.

Taliesin (or Taliesin East as it was later called) was a mythical place for Wright. The landscape around it was that of his forefathers and of his childhood (Wright spent his school holidays working on his uncles' farms); the rolling Wisconsin countryside brought out a shift in his architecture, the forceful horizontal lines of the Prairie houses gradually giving way to something that was altogether softer and more organic – more ancient, too. This period of Wright's work also saw a renewed interest in ornament. Spurred on perhaps by the work of the Viennese Secessionists, his few commissions were intensely decorated, often with motifs drawn from ancient

Native American art. It is as if Taliesin reconnected Wright not only to his own history, but to all history, albeit in a thoroughly modern way.

The first public appearance of this new style was the Midway Gardens (1914) in Chicago. It was designed along the lines of the Austrian beer gardens that Wright had seen in Europe, and became a fashionable meeting place complete with dancefloors and an orchestra pit, as well as vast indoor and outdoor terraces for year-round use. Built of concrete and ceramic tiles, the gardens were a riot of decoration, Wright ornamenting every surface, giving the place the appearance of a rich tapestry alive with patterns and textures. Sadly, the venue's heyday was short-lived: debts mounted, prompting its transformation into a beer garden, but the timing of the whole project was almost comically off, coinciding as it did both with the First World War and the advent of Prohibition. Fifteen years after its creation, the site was closed and the buildings torn down. In something of a backhanded compliment, their structural integrity proved so resilient that the demolition company struggled to raze them and eventually went bankrupt.

The project that sustained Wright through these lean years was the Imperial Hotel in Tokyo (1923). He had visited Japan in 1905, although by then he had been studying and absorbing its distinctive architectural character since at least the World's Columbian Exposition in 1893. When he won the commission to design the Imperial Hotel in 1912, it was a godsend: not only was the project prestigious and complex – the site was next to the Imperial Palace and in a notorious earthquake zone – it also provided him with ongoing work. The hotel is a stunning combination of technical innovation and traditional Japanese design, in keeping with the aim of presenting the country's modernity and ties to the West: the building employed both concrete and (for interior decoration) Ōya, an easily carved igneous stone found only in a small area near the eponymous town in central Japan.

Rather than adopting Japanese design elements throughout, Wright dipped into an ancient architectural aesthetic closer to home: Mayan revival. It's there in the detailed carvings and the overall shape of the structure, which was fashioned after a Mesoamerican pyramid; the style was to become fashionable during the Art Deco years. Fabulously decorated inside and out – right down to the furniture – the Imperial Hotel was one of the few buildings to survive the

Above. Recreation at the Meiji Mura Museum of the interior of the Imperial Hotel, Tokyo, 1923.

Above. Hollyhock House, California, 1921.

disastrous 1923 earthquake thanks to its ingenious flexible foundations, and subsequently earned itself a reputation as a lucky place to get married.

Wright himself was not so lucky in love. In 1914 he hit the headlines again when a servant deliberately set fire to Taliesin East, killing seven people including Mrs Cheney. Unkind critics commented that it was Wright's retribution for abandoning his family for an adulterous relationship. Undeterred, he immediately set about rebuilding Taliesin East, as he did after it burned down a second time in 1924. For all his determination and drive, though, and for all his arrogance and seeming self-confidence, Wright was a man always in need of female admiration and approval. Shortly after Mrs Cheney's death, he embarked on a disastrous relationship with Miriam Noel, a stranger who had written him a letter of condolence. The pair were married but it was not a success: Noel was addicted to morphine and mentally unstable. When Wright began a relationship with Olgivanna Hinzenberg, a Montenegrin dancer and disciple of Russian mystic George Gurdjieff, Noel stalked the couple, had Wright thrown in jail and hounded Olgivanna out of hospital when she gave birth to Wright's seventh child. He divorced Noel in 1927 and married Olgivanna the following year.

While Wright was in Japan working on the Imperial Hotel, another of his projects with a Mayan revival aesthetic was taking shape in Los Feliz, East Hollywood. Built for wealthy heiress Aline Barnsdall, Hollyhock House (1921) has upper walls that tilt back five degrees from the vertical, giving it a faintly ziggurat-like profile. The art-glass panels, furniture, textiles and stonework incorporate a floral motif – a reference to the property's namesake flower, a favourite of the client's.

Barnsdall was a bohemian with a taste for progressive theatre and avant-garde art, and intended the site to become an artists' colony, with a theatre and cinema, accommodation for artists, a pair of guest houses and a residence for her. As Wright was abroad, he employed two rising talents to see the project through: architect Rudolph Schindler and his landscaper friend Richard Neutra. Often seen as a precursor of West Coast modernism, the low-lying, blocky building that resulted proved something of a launch pad for the duo, who went on to create some of Southern California's most outstanding houses.

Barnsdall herself didn't like the place, however. She and Wright argued over its design (as with most of his projects, he demanded creative control) and she was

Above. La Miniatura, California, 1923.

enraged when he went considerably over budget; even then the scheme was left incomplete, with only the main house and two guest houses built by 1921. Disillusioned, she donated the property to Los Angeles. She'd probably warm to it today, though: integrated into the Barnsdall Art Park Foundation, Hollyhock House now includes a performing arts theatre, gallery and artists' studios.

Work was thin on the ground for Wright throughout the 1920s. The Depression coupled with his scandal-ridden private life ensured that few clients came knocking at his door. Anyone else might have retired, but Wright holed up at the ever-expanding Taliesin East and continued to work furiously, churning out endless schemes for buildings that were never built and experimenting with new technologies.

Besides the continuing work in Japan, he built a number of "textile-block" houses in California during this period. These large private residences were

Concrete is a plastic material – susceptible to the impress of the imagination which (if moulded in pieces) is permanent, noble beautiful ... cheap.
Frank Lloyd Wright,
Architectural Record, 1928

constructed using a system of reinforced concrete slabs reminiscent of the simple Froebel blocks of his childhood. Describing the process of designing La Miniatura (1923), the house he created for Alice Millard, Wright explained: "Gradually I unfolded to her the scheme of the textile block-slab house gradually forming in my mind since I got home from Japan. She wasn't frightened by the idea. Not at all."

Perhaps Mrs Millard should have been frightened. For what Wright had come up with was a radically new form of construction that, like so many of his inventions, did not wear altogether well. Intended for easy assembly by a single unskilled labourer, the 40-centimetre (16-inch) square concrete blocks were placed one on top of the other and woven together like a piece of fabric by a system of slender interconnecting steel rods – the warp and weft of the structure.

The largest of his textile-block buildings was another Los Feliz property, the Ennis House (1924). Its huge size (it covers some 560 square metres/6,000 square feet) is made to feel even greater by its terraces and tiered construction, all of which give this hilltop home a monumental quality atypical for a Wright residence and make it feel somewhat out of sync with the horizontally aligned buildings that made his name. Its distinguishing relief ornamentation of recurring patterns, which recalls Emerson's observations on nature's repeating geometries, harks back to pre-Hispanic architecture. With an ambience at once both modern and ancient, the building's unusual character has seen it used as a location in more than eighty movies to date, perhaps most famously *Blade Runner* (1982).

Wright's system had plenty of technical problems; the houses – like so many of his buildings – have needed constant attention. But certainly there is something noble, monumental even, about the textile-block homes. The blocks themselves were either plain or embossed with motifs inspired by nature and the art of the pre-Columbian era, resulting in majestically robust-looking buildings whose façades are animated by stunning abstract decorations.

To help him through the lean times of the 1920s, Wright set up the Taliesin Fellowship – a canny ploy to get students and young architects to pay to come and work for him. In the mid-1930s, his health deteriorating, Wright decided to decamp. The whole entourage – Wright, Olgivanna and students – headed west to the warm desert climate of Arizona where, with the help of the Taliesin fellows, Wright designed and built his third home: the winter residence, Taliesin West (1937). One of its earliest apprentices was Edgar J. Kaufmann Jr., who first introduced his father to Wright's ground-breaking architecture – thereby leading to an invaluable patronage for the architect that helped sustain his career.

Set among desert foothills near Scottsdale, Arizona, Taliesin West would become a retreat for Wright and his family. Wright utilized the surrounding environment both as a source of readily available materials and inspiration. The rubble walls were made from rocks joined together with concrete and sand, leaving their surfaces exposed: "desert masonry", Wright called it. The angularity of the stone buildings mirrors the profile of the McDowell Mountains that envelop the site, while the concrete sprites on the site take their lead from desert cacti. It was textbook sustainable architecture.

To moderate the intense Arizona sun, stretched canvas originally served as the ceilings for Wright's office, the garden room and the drafting room; when these perished under the sunlight's harsh glare, they were replaced with longer-lasting synthetic materials. He also integrated large rocks on which ancient petroglyphs (carvings and etchings) had been inscribed by Native Americans, setting them around the site at prominent locations.

Likewise the colour palette. Although a range of hues inspired by nature are present here, from burnt orange to gold, red was the architect's signature colour, in particular Cherokee red. Actually a variation of similarly warm terracotta hues, this rich, rusty colour can be found, for example, on the upholstery in Taliesin West's gathering areas and the 100-seater pavilion.

Wright was one of the most innovative house designers of the twentieth century, constantly refining his idea of what a home should look like, but his vision was bigger than the individual dwelling. In 1932 he began work on Broadacre City, a blueprint for an ideal way of living. Today Broadacre City seems horribly prophetic: a foretaste of the suburban sprawl that obliterates much of America and the rest of the developed world. But in its time, Wright's masterplan was radical. Taking the car – the new "democratic" form of transport – as his starting point, Wright envisaged most of North America – excluding for some reason New England – divided up into a continuous grid of low-rise regional settlements comprising individual 1-acre (0.4-hectare) lots.

Above. Taliesin West, Arizona, 1937.

The city of the future will be "so greatly different from the ancient city or from any city of today that we will probably fail to recognize its coming as a city at all," Wright wrote in *The Disappearing City* (1932), his first book on city planning. "America needs no help to build Broadacre City. It will build itself, haphazardly." Wright may not have set out to realize Broadacre City but the ideas behind it were incorporated into yet another housing prototype – a series of small suburban homes he designed during the 1930s called the Usonian houses.

Usonian was an adjective that Wright mistook as a neologism coined by Samuel Butler – as a synthesis of "USA" and "Utopia" – to describe an ideal America. In fact, the word first appeared in 1903, in a collection of miscellanea entitled *Here and There in Two Hemispheres*, by James Duff: "We of the United States, in justice to Canadians and Mexicans, have no right to use the title 'Americans' when referring to matters pertaining exclusively to ourselves," Duff insists, suggesting instead "Usonian", derived from an abbreviation of United States of North America.

Wright adopted the term to describe a new type of house in his repertoire, one that anticipated ranch-style abodes: single-storey middle-class homes without servants' quarters, with a single living room in place of the traditional parlour and reception room, and a cantilevered "carport" (a word that he coined himself) instead of stable and garage. Most were modular, to permit greater flexibility. "Form and function are one," Wright declared, twisting Sullivan's famous saying, "Form follows function".

They were intended to provide affordable housing for America's masses, at a time when catalogue firms such as Montgomery Ward and Sears were churning out prefabricated house kits. Wright built twenty Usonian houses in total, although they proved more expensive to build than originally thought and wound up as homes for families who were comfortably well off.

The first true Usonian project to be completed (although La Miniatura anticipates it in spirit) was the Herbert and Katherine Jacobs House (1937) in Madison, Wisconsin. Also known as Jacobs I, to distinguish it from a later property for the same client, it was built for a young journalist and his family. The choice of materials – baked clay bricks, wood, stone – integrated the property within its natural surroundings, with glass curtain walls further dissolving the divide. Bedrooms and living room both have French windows

Above. Fallingwater, Pennsylvania, 1937.

and terraces, opening on to an inner courtyard and nearby garden. It has a
simple L-shaped plan, with living and dining rooms – which are integrated,
anticipating ranch-style housing – along one wing, bedrooms and study along
the other; the kitchen and bathroom sit at the meeting point. The entire thing
is set on a concrete block, beneath which lies piping for underfloor heating.

But the house for which he continues to be best remembered is another
one from this period: Fallingwater. Wright was into his late sixties when Edgar
J. Kaufmann approached him with a new commission in 1934. (He'd been
introduced to Wright's ground-breaking architecture by his son, who had
been one of Taliesin West's earliest apprentices.) Work had picked up a little
but, for an architect of his stature, designing inexpensive middle-class homes
was not ideal. However, when Kaufmann showed him the site at Bear Run,
Pennsylvania, Wright realized this was the project he had been waiting for.
And you have to agree with him.

Dubbed the "most famous house in the world today" by *House and Home*
magazine in 1958, Fallingwater (1937; guesthouse added 1939) was
conceived in a single day. As legend has it, Kaufmann, anxious that he had
seen no drawings or preparatory sketches since their initial visit to the site,

Above. Fallingwater, Pennsylvania, 1937.

met Wright and asked what he was planning. Sitting down, Wright produced the design for Fallingwater straight off.

And yet, it had taken a lifetime to get to Fallingwater. The building is the culmination of Wright's concern to marry architecture and nature and, in so doing, to bring man closer to a spiritual understanding of the world. "I would like to have free architecture," as he famously put it, "Architecture that belongs where you see it standing, and is a grace to the landscape instead of a disgrace."

Glass walls make the surrounding woodland feel immanent, as if they're simply a room next door. Cantilevered over a two-tiered waterfall, the house seems to grow directly out of the rock bed, fanning out in a series of cascading terraces where one can sit and admire the dramatic view. Wright wanted the waterfall to become an integral part of the Kaufmann family's sojourns here, and a hatch in the living room led, via a suspended staircase, to the stream beneath the building. Dispensing with ornament, Wright let the materials speak for themselves. Bringing the outdoor world in, as well as extending the house to the outdoors, he finished the interiors with rough stone walls and flagging so that the whole place feels like the inside of a cave.

In a talk given to the Teliesin Fellowship in 1955, Wright said,

Fallingwater is a great blessing – one of the great blessings to be experienced here on earth, I think nothing yet ever equalled the co-ordination [and] sympathetic expression of the great principle of repose where forest and stream and rock and all the elements of structure are combined so quietly that really you listen not to any noise whatsoever, although the music of the stream is there. But you listen to Fallingwater the way you listen to the quiet of the country.

It is as though the Taliesin East period had been a time of gestation. Thirty years after he first caught the world's attention with his Prairie houses, Wright again achieved worldwide recognition. Fallingwater was hailed as a masterpiece and in 1938 he appeared on the cover of *Time* magazine. In 1941, the Museum of Modern Art in New York dedicated an exhibition to his work. Wright was now well into his late sixties, yet he still had two of his best-known buildings ahead of him: the Johnson Wax headquarters and the Guggenheim Museum.

A friend of Wright's, Herbert Johnson was a wealthy industrialist who had helped fund the Taliesin Fellowship. In 1936, he asked Wright to design a new administration building and laboratories for his family business – the massively successful Johnson Wax Company. Like Fallingwater, the Johnson Wax headquarters (1939, tower added in 1950) is one of the iconic buildings of the twentieth century. The complex – which like so many Wright projects ran staggeringly over budget – was built in two phases: first the ground-hugging administration centre, then the fourteen-storey research tower. As different from each other as it is possible to get, the two buildings form an extraordinary composition, each playing with ideas of transparency: the forest of lily-pad columns in the administration building's Great Workroom supporting a glass roof that brings light cascading down into the windowless interior; the tower, its corners gently rounded, sheathed in horizontal bands of Pyrex glass tubing.

As at Unity Temple, as at the Robie House, Wright injects drama into his scheme by making the entrance a dark, compressed affair, almost tucked away, in order to set up the breathtaking reveal of the double-height splendour of the

Above. Johnson Wax headquarters, Wisconsin, 1950.

Great Workroom. "This building was designed to be as inspiring a place to work in as any cathedral ever was to worship in," Wright said of this uplifting space, in a statement that also evokes the monumental qualities of his Larkin Building.

Those reinforced concrete structural columns at Johnson Wax are self-supporting, requiring no connecting beams. But at a mere 23 centimetres (9 inches) in diameter at their base, swelling to 5.5 metres (18 feet) at their apex, they worried building inspectors and Wright was obliged to prove their weight-bearing capacity; remarkably, a test column could support five times the load specified. The Larkin Building conveyed stability and permanence; the Johnson Wax headquarters is an essay in subtlety, using less to achieve more.

Not all of Wright's Usonian projects were houses. The Unitarian Meeting House (1951) in Madison, Wisconsin, shares with the rest a concrete floor, overhanging eaves and single-storey construction. Its distinguishing feature, however, is the "prow", a forward-thrusting glass-and-wood window that has also been compared to hands folded in worship, sheltered beneath an overhanging angular, seamed-copper roof; immediately inside is the pulpit. It reflects the diamond geometry, derived from the triangle shape, that underpins the overall design of the building. The triangle, Wright noted in *Architectural Forum* the following year, "stands for aspiration ... Here is a church where the whole edifice is in the attitude of prayer." The building had personal resonance for the architect: in 1879, his parents became founding members of the First Unitarian Society of Madison. He was a member of the congregation here and delivered its opening sermon.

The only one of Wright's high-rise designs to be completed in his lifetime was the Price Tower (1956), the headquarters for the H. C. Price oil and chemical firm, located in downtown Bartlesville, Oklahoma. The building was intended as a mixed-use property, combining retail outlets, residential apartments and offices; only the top seven floors were originally devoted to the Price Company itself. It comprises four quadrants and, as with the Johnson Wax laboratory tower, has a tree-like structure. The "trunk" comprises four lift shafts and their respective reinforced concrete structural walls, and extends deep underground to provide the building's anchoring foundation. These four interior walls extend in a cross-shaped spine, branch-like, to support the skyscraper's nineteen concrete cantilevered floors.

The exterior walls feature copper cladding (the "leaves") decorated with geometric patterns; the bluish-green verdigris they have acquired over time only complements the organic theme.

The tower's distinctive silhouette results from a framework that divides every floor into quadrants of varying shape and size, resulting in a pinwheel floor plan based on a grid of thirty- and sixty-degree triangles. It tapers to an apex that accommodates a suite of penthouse rooms originally intended for Harold C. Price himself. Wright's choice of materials was characteristically up to the minute, including aluminium trims for doors and windows, pigmented concrete floors in his favourite Cherokee red and cast-concrete walls.

Wright also designed much of the interior, everything from furnishings, drapery and upholstery to the decorative art, intended (of course) to chime aesthetically with the rest of the building. The apartments had a triangular floor plan, and the same geometry recurs in everything from angular copper-topped tables, to rugs, ceiling lights, air-conditioning vents and to the irregular hexagonal profile of the lifts.

One might ponder how the H. C. Price workforce felt working in such a closely designed environment. Wright was known to visit clients after he'd built their houses, rearranging – "correcting", from his point of view – alterations they'd made to the furniture, or artwork they'd added without his knowledge. Perhaps he always thought of those houses as intrinsically his, given the depth and detail of his design.

When anyone asked Wright which was his greatest building, his reply was always the same: "My next one." So it is fitting that his last building should also be his most famous. As with almost every other project he designed, the Solomon R. Guggenheim Museum (1959) in New York turns conventional forms upside down. In place of rectangular galleries piled on top of one another, Wright created a stunningly abstract edifice. Once again like the Froebel blocks of his childhood, the museum's arresting yellow-buff exterior (later replaced with a light grey) has at its heart a strong geometric element: in this case, a spiralling ramp that forms the main space and serves as a continuous floor, creating a sense of fluidity that had long been inherent in his work.

The structure widens as it rises to a concrete-ribbed translucent glass dome – recalling earlier top-lit projects such as Oak Park's Unity Temple and

Above. Price Tower, Oklahoma, 1956.

It is not to subjugate the paintings to the building that I conceived this plan. On the contrary, it was to make the building and the painting a beautiful symphony such as never existed in the World of Art before. Frank Lloyd Wright, letter to Harry Guggenheim, 1958

the Larkin Building in Buffalo; light also enters from glass strips that top the curving walls. Intriguingly, the concrete façade is non-supportive, being suspended from a structural steel grid. It's thin, too, just 12.7 centimetres (5 inches) deep at some points. Notes in the construction archives warn against using long nails to hang artworks, as there was a risk they could have penetrated through to the exterior.

Wright had toyed with spiral forms since at least the mid-1920s, when he drew up plans for the unbuilt Gordon Strong Automobile Objective, a planetarium and restaurant to be sited on Sugar Loaf Mountain in Maryland, surrounded by a helical ramp for cars. As an architect who revered nature, and came to regard the square as a hard and artificial form, he doubtless enjoyed the sight of his coiled maverick rising up on Museum Mile among New York's stiff rectilinear skyscrapers.

Artists have argued over the merits of the Guggenheim as a space in which to show art since the opening night. Neither was it ideal for art lovers. The ramps obliged them to stand on an incline most of the time, looking at paintings that were tilting away from them. Wright argued that this was closer to the effect of a canvas on an easel, a comment that conveniently ignored the walls' curvature.

In a review for *The New Yorker* published a month after the museum opened, Lewis Mumford dubbed it "a Procrustean structure; the art in it must be stretched out or chopped off to fit the bed Wright prepared for it. The building magnifies Wright's greatest weakness as an architect – the fact that once he fastened on a particular structural form (a triangle, a hexagon, a circle), he imposed it upon every aspect of his design, with no regard for the human purposes it presumably served." Mumford was a friend of some thirty years' standing, and well aware of Wright's shortcomings. And of his importance: a few years earlier, again in *The New Yorker*, he'd praised him as "the most original architect the United States had produced". What is sure, though, is that the Guggenheim is one of the most impressive spaces in architectural history, visited by millions of art lovers every year. It triumphantly transcends its flaws.

Wright died in 1959, just in time to see his masterpiece completed and his place in the history books assured. He is undoubtedly one of the great twentieth-century architects – indeed one of the great architects of all time. Many of his buildings have structural failings, but it is the vision that counts: the vision to break through the rigid box style of nineteenth-century architecture and see that buildings can be so much more complex and fluid, so much more alive with possibility, so much in harmony with their natural environment. At this, Wright excelled. And in his own personal style, in his arrogance and ambition, his irreverence for social conventions, Wright anticipated the rather high-handed behaviour we have come to expect of today's architects. He may not be the greatest architect of all time, but he's up there.

Above. A model of the unbuilt Gordon Strong Automobile Objective, on display at the Guggenheim Museum in New York. **Overleaf.** William Winslow House, Illinois, 1894.

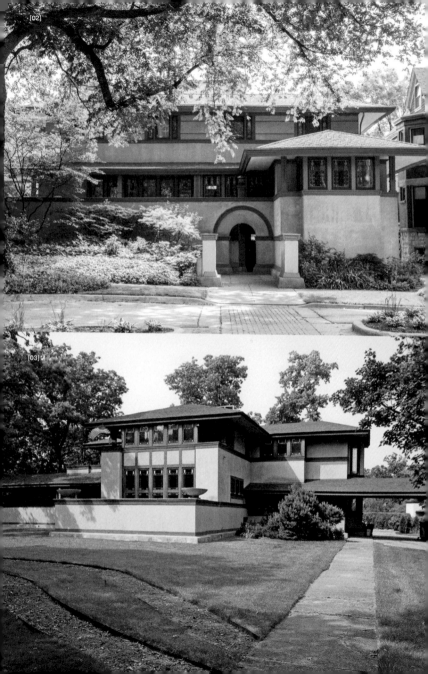

[01] Frank Lloyd Wright Home and Studio, Illinois, 1889. [02] Frank Thomas House, Illinois, 1901. [03] Ward Willits House, Illinois, 1901. [04] Dana–Thomas House, Illinois, 1904.

[05] Martin House, New York, 1905. [06] Stockman House, Iowa, 1908. [07] Boynton House, New York, 1908.

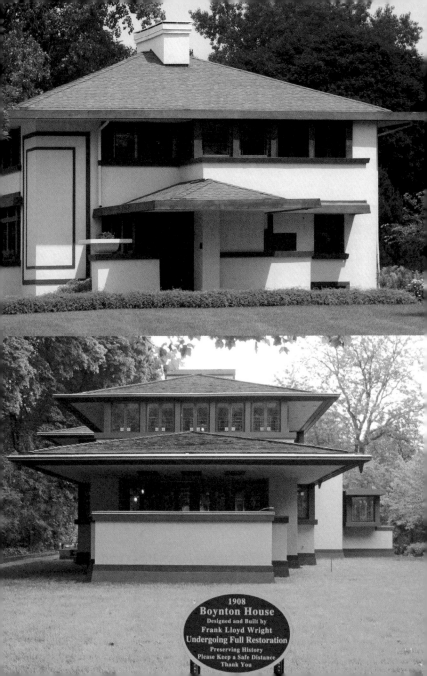

1908
Boynton House
Designed and Built by
Frank Lloyd Wright
Undergoing Full Restoration
Preserving History
Please Keep a Safe Distance
Thank You

[08] Unity Temple, Illinois, 1908. [09] Park Inn Hotel, Iowa, 1910. [10] Hollyhock House, California, 1921.

[12]

[11] Recreation at the Meiji Mura Museum of the Imperial Hotel, Tokyo, 1923. [12, 13] Ennis House, California, 1924. [14, 15] Westhope (or Richard Lloyd Jones House), Oklahoma, 1929.

[16] Graycliff Estate, New York, 1931. [17] Hanna–Honeycomb House, California, 1937.
[18] Fallingwater, Pennsylvania, 1937. [19] Jacobs House I, Wisconsin, 1937.

[20, 21] Taliesin West, Arizona, 1937. [22, 23] Johnson Wax headquarters, Wisconsin, 1939 (tower added in 1950).

[24, 25, 26] Wingspread (Johnson House), Wisconsin, 1939. [27, 28] Pope–Leighey House, Virginia, 1940. [29] V. C. Morris Gift Store, California, 1949. [30] Unitarian Meeting House, Wisconsin, 1951. [31] Cedar Rock (Lowell Walter House), Iowa, 1950.

[32] Zimmerman House, New Hampshire, 1951. [33] Laurent House, Illinois, 1952.
[34, 35] Bachman–Wilson House, New Jersey, 1956.

[36, 37, 38] Kentuck Knob, Pennsylvania, 1956. [39, 40, 41] Beth Sholom Synagogue, Pennsylvania, 1959.

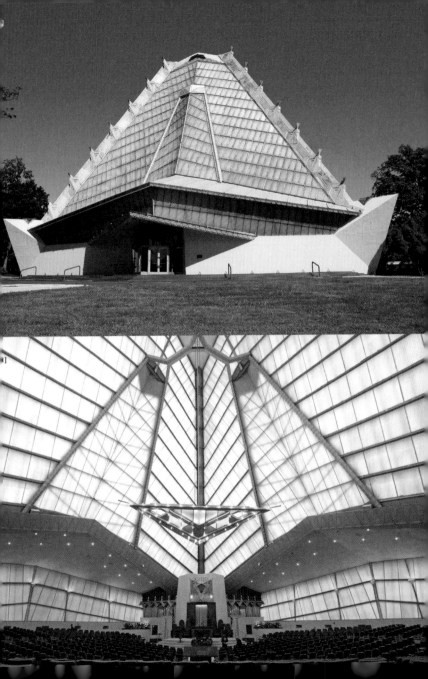

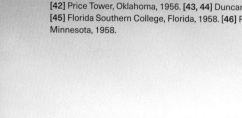

[42] Price Tower, Oklahoma, 1956. [43, 44] Duncan House, Illinois, 1957.
[45] Florida Southern College, Florida, 1958. [46] R. W. Lindholm Service Station,
Minnesota, 1958.

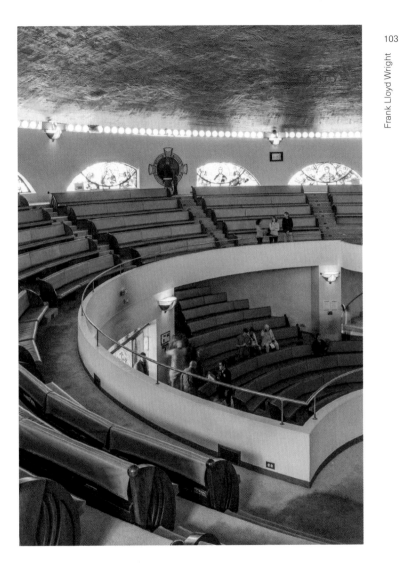

[47, 48, 49] Solomon R. Guggenheim Museum, New York, 1959. [50] Rudin House, Wisconsin, 1959. [51, 52] Annunciation Greek Orthodox Church, Wisconsin, 1961.